KB GAMEPLAN
Kingdom Builders Devotional

Lee Domingue

Kingdom Builders Publishing

This book is dedicated to:

My first spiritual father, Pastor Curry Juneau,
who always taught me to believe God gives second chances.

CONTENTS

INTRODUCTION

Many years ago, I was at a very dry place in my spiritual life. I just wanted to give up. I did not want to pray or read my bible. Needless to say, I was not hearing from God. A close friend of mine was going through incredible personal pain and loss. It genuinely felt like we were experiencing some of the pain, as we were very close to him.

Before that happened, I had decided I was going to start writing a second book. A weekly devotional book, for businesspeople that was based in God's Word, simple, transparent and practical. It was a struggle as I started, and it just was not happening. It took me an entire year to write 11 (yes, I know, not even one devotional a month)!

A pastor friend of mine from another city reached out to me and offered (kind of demanded) we use his church's retreat house in Tennessee. It was a beautiful place, and its sole purpose was for people to rest, recalibrate and reconnect with God. My wife and I reluctantly agreed, and decided our time there would be January 1st of the New Year.

Once we got to our destination, we were blown away by the serenity of the place. We settled in the house and began our time of searching. We talked for hours by the fireplace. We laughed, we cried as we reflected on our lives, our kids, our regrets, and what our future held. When you are fasting from food it's amazing how much time you have!

My prayer time with God was a bit awkward the first day and even the second day. We were committed to continue. It began to snow outside and kept us in the house most of the time. It was that day God spoke to me in a way I have never experienced before. I was crying out to God in a place of brokenness and vulnerability, and God met me in my pain. As I look back it was really a heavenly download. In a span of just 3 to 4 hours, I started to get thoughts for devotional titles and scripture references that validated them. Later that day, as I reviewed my journal notes, I sensed the Lord say to me, "it can be like this all the time son if you will take time to turn off the noise of the world, stop looking at your situation and spend some time with me."

I was marked that day and the result of that time with God is this Kingdom Builder Weekly Devotional book. You are about to take a one-year journey. I hope after reading each week's devotional, you will never be the same.

"Then you will call on me and come and pray to me, and I will listen to you. You will seek me and find me when you seek me with all your heart." Jeremiah 29:12-13 (NIV)

Believing for God's best,

Lee Domingue
Kingdom Builder since 2001

WEEK 1:
CLEAR DIRECTION

Your Word is a lamp for my feet and a light for my path.
Psalm 119:105 (NIV)

The secret to success for every Kingdom Builder, and for every single believer, is to love the Word of God. And by this, I don't simply mean that we have a warm fuzzy feeling on the inside about the things Jesus said. I am referring to an honest-to-goodness, authentic relationship with the Word, where we actually read the Bible every day and meditate on it day and night.

For a person to call himself a Christian, but to never spend time in the Word is like someone packed to go on a long journey without a map. He'd set off, excited for the trip, but very soon after departure, he'd have no idea where he was or even how to get from point A to point B. And if opposition came against him, he would not know how to navigate through the difficulties. In the end, he would never get to his desired destination.

As Kingdom Builders, we must make a choice to love and obey God's Word. It is the Truth that will guide us through ANY circumstance: in marriage, in parenting, in business, in relationships, in our emotions, in our finances, in everything. It is only through God's Word that we can come to know God and His Son, Jesus. And really, it's the only way we will come to know our true selves. The Word works as a mirror in our lives, reflecting our gifts and talents as well as teaching us the motives of everything we do. It is only through the Word that we grow into the kind of mature Christians that will be able to impact the world around us.

I encourage you to dive deeply into God's Word today. And don't simply read a few verses out of obligation, ask God to help you to love His Word. He will put a fire into your heart that will give you the power and the desire to read and to meditate on His Word daily. You'll never be the same again!

NOTES

WEEK 2:
GOD'S WAYS ARE NOT OUR WAYS

In his heart a man plans his course,
but the LORD determines his steps.
Proverbs 16:9 (NIV)

Most people in our world are searching desperately for true meaning and significance in their lives. Even for many believers, we struggle with thoughts and insecurities, wondering if how we are spending our days will matter in the end. Once we have walked into eternity, will the things we attempted to achieve make any impact on the world we left?

I have good news for you today. If you will allow God to determine every step of your life, in your marriage and family, in your businesses, and in your Kingdom Building, then you can rest assured that your life will be filled with the favor and prosperity of the Almighty God.

Remember, God does not see "success" as most people see it. He does not value or honor the standards the world believes to be the most important. And so, as a Kingdom Builder, you must come to know God in such an intimate way that you begin to view your success and the course of your destiny through His eyes. That you learn to value what GOD values. Otherwise, if you chase after the same things the world runs after, you will waste your time orchestrating the wrong game plan for your life. You'll exhaust your time and energy on exploits that might build your own ego, but not the Kingdom of God.

Be a KINGDOM BUILDER, not an ego builder. Submit your plans to the Lord, and allow Him to determine your steps. Better yet, completely submit your heart to the Lord so that He can guide your thoughts to become agreeable to His will. Only then will ALL your plans succeed!

NOTES

WEEK 3:
WHAT ARE YOU CHASING?

Seek first the Kingdom of God, and His righteousness,
and all these things shall be added unto you.
Matthew 6:33 (NKJV)

As pastors and marketplace leaders, we are wired with great vision. Deep in our souls, we are energized by the accomplishment of great exploits and we feel energized when there is a challenge before us to attack...and WIN! But even deeper in our spirits, we are motivated by the call of God on our lives, and the intense desire to be influential ambassadors for Jesus Christ.

One of the most common pitfalls for a Kingdom Builder is that we can get too busy achieving things for God. We are so full of strategies for reaching the lost, so preoccupied with the busyness of building our businesses and our churches, we forget about God. We don't have time to pray, we don't have time to go to church; in fact, we don't even have time to stop and make sure all our "good" plans are actually "God" plans which have His blessing.

It's time to stop chasing all the rabbits. If you are feeling worn out, irritated, worried, or anxious...then I'm talking to you right now. Remember the Proverb that says, "The blessing of the Lord makes one rich, and He adds no sorrow to it." If you are dealing with the sorrows of a life that is too full of what you are calling the "blessings" of God, then guess what? It's time to clean out your schedule and get back to the only thing that matters: Seeking FIRST the Kingdom of God.

When we are diligent to seek God's face FIRST, over everything else, it is amazing how much clarity and rest our hearts can experience. We will begin to see those aspects of our ministry and business that we've allowed to become out of balance. And maybe even notice some exploits that were never God-breathed in the first place. In His presence, He will reveal to us what He has for us to do and to accomplish. And then we must be disciplined to do ONLY those things. The end.

Don't allow your destiny to be diluted by distraction. Seek the face of God. Allow Him, and Him only, to direct your steps.

NOTES

WEEK 4:
GOD CALLS THE UNQUALIFIED

The Lord is with you, you mighty man of valor! Go in this
might of yours, have I not sent you?
Judges 6:12,14 (NKJV)

I love the story of Gideon. Here's a guy who is hiding from everyone, including God, who is afraid of everyone, and who believes he is a nobody going nowhere. And it's in this state that the Angel of the Lord comes to him and greets him by calling him "a mighty man of valor." I don't know about you, but this is deeply encouraging to me. Even when we are in our lowest places, God still sees us through His eyes of faith.

There are so many pearls of wisdom that can be drawn from Gideon's life, but today I want to emphasize this point: It's not your job to qualify yourself for the plan God has called you to execute. It is GOD who qualifies you. He doesn't scrutinize where you are at the moment to determine how successful you will become. And thankfully, He doesn't consult your past to decide what He wants for your future.

Just like with Gideon, God has a plan for your life that is beyond your wildest dreams. Before the foundations of the earth were laid, He mapped out for you a life filled with good works and a future that is full of hope and promise. He has called you to be a king, and He needs you to help rally behind His Cause to build His Kingdom. However, it's up to you to pick up the crown He has waiting for you.

It's OK if you have doubts about yourself and about your ability. No one was in need of a self-esteem adjustment more than Gideon, but God called him anyway. Fortunately, Gideon answered the call (shaking in his boots most of the time), God showed up just like He said He would, and Gideon achieved great exploits. You can read all about his amazing life in Judges 6.

Stop focusing on your inferiority and start focusing on God's superiority! Put your trust in Him, and believe that through you He will accomplish every single thing He has promised. Allow God to be your plan and to be your provision. He will never let you down, and you will experience a life filled with more blessing than you could have ever asked or imagined!

NOTES

WEEK 5:
NO MAN AN ISLAND

A man who isolates himself seeks his own desire;
he rages against all sound judgment.
Proverbs 18:1 (NKJV)

Kingdom Builders, we must understand that the quality of our success in every area of life will be dependent upon the quality of our relationships. Any king who thinks he can fulfill his destiny without several strong, intimate relationships is a fool. I cannot put it any plainer than that.

We were made in the likeness and image of God (Genesis 1:26) and God is a relationship! Think about it: He is the Father, the Son, and the Holy Spirit. So in essence, although all three are one, they are still each a distinct and unique Person, each engaged in a relationship with each other. It's a mystery, and difficult to wrap our minds around, but that doesn't make it less true. The very thing that makes God God is relationship. In addition, when God walked on this planet, He was all about relationships. Jesus cherished His time with the 3 (Peter, James, and John), with the 12 Apostles, and with the 70 who were mentored by Him, and sometimes even were sent out into ministry. If Jesus needed the support and comradery of friends, how much more do we?

Every Kingdom Builder must make it a priority to build, and to nurture vulnerable and God-centered relationships. These people around you will sharpen you, keep you accountable, and inspire you to be all you can be. They will be there to celebrate your greatest victories, and to support you through your toughest trials. Make it a point today to reach out and nurture the God-given relationships in your life.

NOTES

WEEK 6:
THE DIFFERENCE MAKER

And I will ask the Father, and He will give you another Comforter
(Counselor, Helper, Intercessor, Advocate, Strengthener, and
Standby), that He may remain with you forever.
John 14:16-17 (AMP)

This is one of the most beautiful and significant promises Jesus ever made to us. Here Jesus is revealing the very culmination of His life, death and resurrection. God so passionately loved us that it was not sufficient for Him to merely have a close relationship with us, He wanted to actually abide within us. And because of Jesus' death and resurrection, God has made Himself available to every believer, through the Holy Spirit, and will actually live on the inside of our hearts. In the light of this revelation, how could anyone not receive such an invaluable and precious gift?

The most important relationship any believer can have is with the Holy Spirit. And as men and women who are passionate to build the Kingdom of God, this relationship is absolutely vital. Our God-sized success of the God-inspired dreams within our hearts are entirely dependent upon the work of the Holy Spirit.

And, yes, I am saying that on your own, you don't have what it takes to live in the fullness God has for you. And while this might be ego-shattering for you, it is crucial you come to realize this truth.

Take it from me, because I lived a portion of my life without the power of the Holy Spirit, and I was on the fast-track to destruction. My life was like a high performance 12-cylinder sports car running on 2-cylinders. It had all the potential, but none of the power. I was trapped in cycles of sin that were destroying my life, and I had no real power to break those strongholds. It was not until I experienced the authentic power of the Holy Spirit living inside of me that I was able to see real and lasting change.

I urge you to tap into the tremendous power of the Holy Spirit. He is waiting for you and fully available to you. He will counsel you, strengthen you, help you, and lead and guide you. His peace will guide your every step, and His wisdom will whisper in your heart the things that are to come. The Holy Spirit is God's American Express Card. Don't leave home without Him!

NOTES

WEEK 7:
THE FULLNESS OF ONENESS

Two are better than one, because they have a good reward for their labor. For if they fall, one will lift up his companion. But woe to him who is alone when he falls, for he has no one to help him up...
And a threefold cord is not quickly broken.
Ecclesiastes 4:9-10,12 (NKJV)

Have you ever stopped to think about the fact that marriage was God's idea? No sooner had our Father created man, then He declared, "It is not good for man to be alone," and he established marriage! And since that time until now, marriage has been the very thumbprint of God upon all of humanity. In every society, every nation, in every season of history, in prosperity, in slavery and oppression, there has always been a man seeking to share his life with a woman. Think about the significance of that for a minute.

Marriage is a powerful, powerful union, no wonder Satan has tried every which way to wreak havoc upon it. As kings, our spouse is the most important, most influential and most rewarding human relationship we will every encounter. This partnership will make or break our success as Kingdom Builders. Our husband or wife is our mirror, our partner, and the other half of our God-given destiny. It's time for all believers to grasp this truth and honor marriage as the holy institution God created it to be. And if you are single right now, be assured that God, who has you in the palm of His hands, is preparing an amazing spouse for you. In the meantime, Jesus Himself will be your partner.

It is a fight to have a healthy marriage, but let me assure you, the rewards of a strong marriage are worth every bit of the fight. Just as the scripture above states, 'a threefold cord is not quickly broken.' How awesome is it to understand that the 3rd chord is Jesus Christ Himself?! When two people come together, and the union is Christ centered, no power in hell can come against the strength of that agreement. I don't know about you, but I want to live every day in that kind of power!

NOTES

WEEK 8:
THE KINGS MEN (or Women)

*He who walks with wise men will be wise, But the
companions of fools will experience harm.*
Proverbs 13:20 (AMP)

Every Kingdom Builder needs relationships: mentors, brothers, sisters and partners in destiny. If you think you can circumvent this truth, let me tell you, you are in for one long and lonely ride. And while I realize building strong friendships and business partnerships can be difficult, and sometimes even very painful, it is essential we spend the time doing so.

I have to admit, there have been times in my life when I was the latter part of this famous proverb—associating with fools—and I paid dearly for those immature choices. But I became determined to learn from my mistakes, and today, I am extremely grateful for the incredible men and women of God in my inner circle of friends who are like-minded. Brothers and sisters who have a global vision to win souls for Christ and to build the Kingdom of God.

The greatest pearl of wisdom I have found for establishing and building intimate relationships is this: use patience and diligent prayer. The people we choose to co-labor with in life have the access to influence our thoughts, our emotions, our actions and our very destinies. We must be very careful in our selection. Only God knows the hearts of men. So it is only through prayer that we can hear His wisdom about the individuals He wants each of us to link arms with.

Look for friends who love unconditionally, but who speak the truth when needed. Stay away from those who are striving, always critical of others, and who have a spirit of comparison about them. And don't forget to BE the kind of friend you are looking for. Be very shrewd when picking the people who will become part of your inner circle of friends. And once they are chosen, love them back, be loyal to a fault, and never try to change them into something they are not. As a result, you will experience the fullness of what God has designed for you, and you will truly have people around you "doing life" with you!

NOTES

WEEK 9:
YOUR POWER SOURCE

But you will receive power when the Holy Spirit comes upon you.
And you will be my witnesses, telling people about
me everywhere—in Jerusalem, throughout Judea,
in Samaria, and to the ends of the earth.
Acts 1:8 (NLT)

If you were saying good-bye to a person whom you greatly admired and loved, and you knew that the words they were about to say to you would be the very last ones you'd ever hear from them, you'd take note of them, wouldn't you? How much more should every believer cherish and ponder upon the last instructions Jesus Christ spoke before being taken up into heaven?

"You shall receive power when the Holy Spirit comes upon you," and THEN you will make an impact upon the world around you. Jesus even told them to wait in Jerusalem and not to do any evangelizing of any kind UNTIL the Holy Spirit came upon them. He said this because He knew that in order for each of them to have the internal fortitude, wisdom and power to fulfill the call of God on their lives, they were going to need something (or Someone) more than their own ability.

Every day, I thank God for His Holy Spirit working in me. Every. Single. Day. Because I know all the aspects of my life I deem as successful, I could NOT have accomplished without His power and wisdom working through me.

Dis Louisiana Cajun boy just ain't dat smart! And the only way YOU are going to accomplish all the God-sized dreams on the inside of you is by leaning into the God-sized Holy Spirit power that is available to you.

But you might say, I don't know if I'm good enough or smart enough to do anything great for God. Listen, the VERY SAME Holy Spirit that worked inside Jesus can work through you! It's the same Holy Spirit that has allowed our modern day heroes like Martin Luther King, Jr., Billy Graham, or Joyce Meyer to influence their world. All you have to do is ask God to connect you with the Holy Spirit, to be able to discern His voice in your heart, and to walk in His power. As a Kingdom Builder, your heart is to impact the world around you. You can do it, but you're going to need the Holy Spirit.

NOTES

WEEK 10:
THE DISCIPLINE OF INTIMACY

Don't let the wise boast in their wisdom, or the powerful
in their power, or the rich in their riches.
But those who wish to boast should boast in this alone:
That they truly know Me and understand that I am the Lord...
Jeremiah 9:23-24 (NLT)

God yearns for intimacy with us; it was the very reason He created us. He wants to make His home in our hearts and to share a give-and-take relationship of thoughts, feelings, visions and dreams. Too often we, as Kingdom Builders, are so busy in the pursuit to accomplish great things for God that we forget about the thing He cares about the most: being with us.

We are men and women of action, we set our goals high, and are focused and disciplined to achieve them. If our relationship with God could be based on our activities and accomplishments, we would all be enjoying a strong and intimate relationship with our Father in heaven. But this is not what God desires from us. He deeply desires to be a part of our lives, involved in our thought processes, and above all, King of our hearts.

Nothing can substitute an authentic and intimate relationship with our God. In fact, intimacy with God should be the #1 discipline of every Kingdom Builder. In His presence is where you find your vision, your direction and your faith in His Word and His promises. It is here you find courage to take the risks required to fulfill your deepest dreams, it is here you find your self-esteem, your value, your meaning. It is here you begin to fathom the unconditional love God has for you.

This week, carve out time in your schedule to spend some daily one-on-one time with God. He's waiting to breathe life into your heart and refresh your soul like never before. Even if it's just 10 minutes, it'll be the best 10 minutes of your day, and before you know it, it will grow into more!

NOTES

WEEK 11:
COMPARISON.... THE DREAM KILLER

For we dare not class ourselves or compare ourselves with those who commend themselves. But they, measuring themselves by themselves, and comparing themselves among themselves, are not wise.
2 Corinthians 10:12 (NKJV)

There is nobody who wins the game of comparison, so why do we all play it? For some of us, we compare ourselves against those who have made smaller accomplishments than us, because we want to feel better about ourselves. For some of us, we compare ourselves against those who have done greater exploits because we are feeling sorry for ourselves. And some of us do both at the same time!

The Apostle Paul was clear that those who compare themselves among themselves are not wise. There is absolutely no accuracy in it! All this does is cause pride to abound and dissatisfaction to flood our hearts. And ultimately, comparison will distract us from staying focused on the individual call God has on each of our lives.

God wants YOU to be YOU. His anointing for your life will only flow through the authentic you anyway. The moment you try to be "as good" as someone else, or you decide to accomplish something God has not purposed for you to do, life becomes hard, overwhelming, and full of anxiety. But when you are simply keeping your eyes on Jesus, happy to do the things He has asked you to do, His anointing will flow through you, and there is an ease and comfort to your work.

And if you must compare yourself to something, compare yourself against the Word of God. There you will find strength, perfect wisdom, and clarity for your God-given destiny. Be a Kingdom Builder who is wise... never allow yourself to fall into the comparison trap!

NOTES

WEEK 12:
ELIMINATING DISTRACTIONS

*Now these are the ones sown among thorns; they are the ones who
hear the word, and the cares of this world, the deceitfulness of
riches, and the desires for other things entering in choke the word,
and it becomes unfruitful.*
Mark 4:18-19 (NKJV)

The Parable of the Sower is one of Jesus' most famous parables, and it's packed with profound pearls of wisdom for every believer to mine out. Today, I want to focus on the third of the four different types of people Jesus referred to in this parable, because I think this one describes many believers in the Body of Christ today.

Here, Jesus is talking about a person who hears the Word and who applies that Word to his life to the point that he brings forth good fruit. But when the cares and deceits of the world begin to crowd into his life, those thorns start to choke out the Word and his life becomes unfruitful.

Kingdom Builders, we must not let ourselves become deceived. The greatest joy of the enemy would be to distract us from our call to build God's Kingdom by turning our hearts away from God. And turn instead, onto greed, lust, anxiety, fear, success, or any other thing that would take the place of God in our lives.

Thorns are ANYTHING that would distract us from God, from spending time with Him, and from fulfilling His purposes for our lives. Take some time today to be brutally honest with yourself. Quietly go before God and ask Him to search your heart to see if there is anything in your life that is crowding Him out. Is there anything that you are putting first before Him? And if He graciously reveals something to you, be diligent to make the needed changes.

God is a jealous God, and He wants to be FIRST in your life. And remember the promise in Matthew 6: when we seek Him first, all His blessings will follow!

NOTES

WEEK 13:
THE WEAPON OF PATIENCE

Therefore, be patient, brethren, until the coming of the Lord. See how the farmer waits for the precious fruit of the earth, waiting patiently for it until it receives the early and latter rain. You also be patient. Establish your hearts, for the coming of the Lord is at hand.
James 5:7-8 (NKJV)

Patience. Just the thought of the word can make some of us cringe inside. We Kingdom Builders are visionaries and dreamers, and we are people who know how to make things happen...YESTERDAY. The last thing we want to do is wait. I cannot tell you how many times my impatience has aborted opportunities that otherwise would have been great blessings from God. It's taken me a long time to learn how to truly be patient, and wait on God's timing for His plans and purposes to come to pass. However, learning this lesson has truly paid off.

Years ago, a company I started had reached a level of success and was attracting larger companies to make bids of purchase. One was offering a very large sum, and most of the details of their offer were very appealing. The only problem was; I didn't have peace about it. I felt like God was asking me to "just wait." This was a tough call because I really didn't think we'd get another offer as lucrative as this one.

I'm so glad I allowed patience to do its work because after months of waiting, red flags began to surface and we passed up the offer. Months later an international company made a bid that not only had the exact terms we were looking for, but was multiple times the amount of the previous company! And because of patience, this put me in a financial position to help my church when it desperately needed it to get a new building funded and completed. I could not have foreseen the timing of this need, but God did.

We are KINGDOM Builders, and when we use patience as a weapon, we will be put in positions to bless God's Church and the generations to come. The first offer would've blessed my family and me, but the second offer did that AND allowed me to significantly bless my local church. Learn to be patient and you will truly be used to glorify God!

NOTES

WEEK 14:
SHINE YOUR LIGHT

Let your light shine before men that they may see your
good works and glorify your Father in heaven.
Matthew 5:16 (NKJV)

Let your light shine. It's one of the first scriptures we memorize as children. As adults, we hear this and think, Yeah, yeah, yeah. Shine my light. Got it. But do you get it? Are you truly shining your light? I think if we emphasize a word in this scripture, it could have a renewed meaning for us: Let YOUR light shine before men. Not your pastor's light, not that guy-who-always-seems-to-get-it-right's light, but YOUR light.

God created you unique from any other individual, with your own skill set, your own quirks, your own spiritual gifts, and your own charisma. Are you being the best YOU...you can be, or are you spending a ton of energy trying to be more like someone else? Are you living out the dreams YOU have deep in your heart, or are you pursuing goals you feel are "better" or that you feel are expected of you?

Henry David Thoreau once said, "Most men lead lives of quiet desperation and go to the grave with the song still in them." He saw people around him living day by day as survivors, never quite rising above the level of mediocrity and never finishing or fulfilling the purpose of their creation.

Don't let this be you. You be YOU. Better yet, be the GOD'S BEST you! Never allow people around you to rob you of your dreams or silence the song God has called you to sing. Do you want to be a Kingdom Builder? Then build His Kingdom by glorifying Him through YOUR works as you live out the God- given destiny He has purposed just for you. When you live confidently, boldly and unapologetically for who you are, you will free others to do the same. They will see your life and have the courage to be who God has called them to be, too. In addition, the world will be drawn to you, asking, "What is it that you have that makes you live life so freely?" And you will be able to share the message of Jesus with them.

Sing your song. The world needs you to sing it. The church needs you to sing it. YOU need to sing it!

NOTES

WEEK 15:
NO SHAME

Instead of their shame my people will receive a double portion,
and instead of disgrace they will rejoice in their inheritance;
and so they will inherit a double portion in their land,
and everlasting joy will be theirs.
Isaiah 61:7 (NIV)

Everyone makes mistakes. Let me say that again: Everyone makes mistakes. We have all done something that we wish we wouldn't have. Some mistakes are big, some are small, some are private, and others are very public. But we've all known the sting of failure. And what comes to many of us afterwards? A greater sting of shame.

Many times throughout scripture, Satan is referred to as "the accuser." It's like he sits and watches for the moment we sin so that he can pile as much shame on our souls as possible. In fact, shame is one of the enemy's top ways to keep a person in bondage and in habitual sin. In fact, I believe shame is like a cancer to man's masculinity and success as a believer. I know this personally because I have had to deal with this in my own life.

Early on in my career, I experienced a failed business that was very public, and shortly after, I privately dealt with failures in relationships that brought much pain. I was plagued with shameful thoughts about what the people around me were thinking of me. But God wanted me healed and set free of all that. Most of all, He wanted me in a place where I no longer looked to man for affirmation, but only came to Him for my self-worth. This scripture became a lifeline for my soul as I confessed it day in and day out for many years, and God was faithful to His Word. More than faithful; "doubly portioned" faithful!

You or someone you know might be in bondage and the spirit of shame is a controlling factor in your life. Let me encourage you today: don't believe the lies of the enemy. It's NEVER too late for God to redeem whatever has been lost! In fact, when you surrender your sin to Him, He will not only give you the courage to release the weights of shame, but He will also fill you with HOPE. Hope for renewed dreams and visions, hope for change, and hope for a double portion of everlasting joy.

Don't let another day of living under the bondage of shame go by. Instead, give God your shame and receive from Him his love and forgiveness. It is only then that you will discover true freedom.

NOTES

WEEK 16:
THE FLOURISHING KING

The [uncompromisingly] righteous shall flourish like the palm
tree [be long-lived, stately, upright, useful, and fruitful];
they shall grow like a cedar in Lebanon [majestic, stable,
durable, and incorruptible]. Planted in the house of
the Lord, they shall flourish in the courts of our God.
Psalm 92:12-13 (AMP)

Majestic. Stable. Durable. Fruitful. These are words every Kingdom Builder would like said of his life, his marriage, his family, and his ministry. Who wouldn't? Even the marketplace leaders in the world seek to find the fruits of these words manifested in their lives.

However, the only people on this planet who will truly flourish, not just in their careers, but also in every other aspect of their lives—relationally, emotionally, and spiritually—are the ones who are planted in the house of the Lord. In other words, they are people who are dedicated to a local church, deeply rooted in service and commitment.

When Jesus walked on earth, He made a powerful statement in the Gospel of Matthew, Chapter 16. He said, "I came to build my Church, and the gates of hell shall not prevail against it." Friend, it is vital that we understand the significance of these words. Jesus said the gates of hell shall not prevail against the church. He did not say that the gates of hell would not prevail against your family, or your business, or your destiny. In other words, just being a Christian does not magically qualify you for this blessing. It is only when you are part of His Church, engaged in your local church, giving and serving and richly rooted in that body, do you experience this blessing.

An authentic Kingdom Builder knows this to the core. And also realizes that the success of his marriage, family, and business is directly related to his love for and his involvement in his local church. Are you under the covering of a local church? And I don't mean you sit home on Sundays and watch Christian TV or live-stream a service. I mean that you actually drive to a church, walk in the building, and interact with other humans! Don't let the enemy deceive you and rob you of your full destiny. Get planted in a great church today!

NOTES

WEEK 17:
ABUNDANCE FOR THE KINGDOM

And God is able to make all grace abound toward you,
that you, always having all sufficiency in all things,
may have an abundance for every good work.
2 Corinthians 9:8 (NKJV)

I'll never forget the day this scripture jumped off the page and exploded into my heart. Laura and I were in a season of life where we were prospering abundantly, and we had more than enough finances to provide for family. In addition, we were also beginning to experience the joy of giving generously to build the Kingdom. I felt like our lives had reached a perfect balance in the financial realm, until this day.

God began to work in my heart about the difference between "sufficiency" and "abundance." Notice the wording in the scripture above. It says God will give us sufficiency for all our needs and abundance for every good work. In other words, sufficiency for me, my family, and all my endeavors, and abundance for every good work God has planned for me to do. I began to realize that we were not as balanced in this area as I thought we were.

You see, our church was right in the middle of a building project, and although we had been faithful to give large amounts toward it, we had been feeling an aching in our hearts, wishing we could do more. As I meditated on this scripture, I began to see just how much of our resources were tied in personal possessions. If we made the choice to trim some of that fat, we would be able to help our church in a more generous way.

Now before half of you freak out, thinking I'm asking you to take a vow of poverty, while the other half of you are willing to empty out your 401K. STOP FOR A SECOND and just talk to God about a balance in this. Obviously, our Father in Heaven wants His children to prosper and be blessed. But what He doesn't want is for us to turn that prosperity upon ourselves, forgetting why He gave it to us in the first place. This is why our intimacy with God must always be a priority in our lives. Knowing the balance of "sufficiency" vs. "abundance" is a matter of the heart. Only God can draw the line in the sand for you.

Remember, we are Kingdom Builders. We are not here to build our own personal kingdoms, but to build an everlasting Kingdom!

NOTES

WEEK 18:
CLEAN BUSINESS

But as He who called you is holy, you also be holy in all your conduct, because it is written, "Be holy, for I am holy."
1 Peter 1:15-16 (NKJV)

For many of us leaders in the marketplace, we are keenly aware that running a clean business these days is something like an oxymoron. And by "clean," I'm not simply referring to the finances reconciling perfectly; I'm talking about every aspect of our business life. Operating with honor and integrity: staffing, human relations, accounting, hiring and firing...the whole gambit!

But if we are to call ourselves Kingdom Builders, then shouldn't everything we aim to accomplish be built on Kingdom principles, on God's holy Word? What kind of a testimony is it for us to give richly to help finance the work of God in our local churches, and yet behind-the-scenes in our business, we're known as a Scrooge or a shyster? Or what kind of legacy is it to be publicly lauded as a philanthropist, but privately our marriage and our family is in shambles?

As a Kingdom Builder, we must understand that God is profoundly more concerned about who we are than about what we do. He desires for each of us to be holy in every area, because it is only by walking out our lives with integrity and love that we can truly glorify His Name. This is the way we build God's Kingdom and leave a great legacy for the next generation.

Spend some time today, quietly before your Father, and ask Him how you are doing in this area. He is such a tender Father, and He will show you aspects of your heart that you've allowed to become unholy: fearful or anxious worries, dishonest actions or speech, lustful thoughts, or even simply laziness or procrastination. Remember, God is not looking for perfection from you. Just a heart that desires to be clean before Him!

NOTES

WEEK 19:
TIME FOR GOD

Blessed are those who dwell in Your presence;
they will be singing Your praises all the day long.
Psalm 84:4 (AMP)

Time is a precious commodity. Every person is given the same amount each day along with the choice to use it wisely or to squander it away; but once it's gone, it's gone forever. Successful business and ministry leaders understand how valuable time is, and how important it is to wisely manage it each and every day. Especially in today's society where distractions seem to come at us from all sides.

So how does a Kingdom Builder do it? I'm asked this question in almost every Q&A Session I'm in. How do you juggle the schedule, the business, the meetings, the marriage, the kids' sporting events, church, and countless other commitments, and still have time left over to spend with God?

My answer is almost always the same: I always have time "left over" for God because I never give Him my leftovers. The only way I have been able to manage my time wisely throughout my walk as a Christian husband, dad, friend, marketplace leader, and Kingdom Builder, is by putting time with God first. When I make my relationship with God my utmost priority, I have literally been shocked at how He, in turn, has multiplied the remaining hours of my day! Sometimes He's given me wisdom about how to accomplish things in half the time. Sometimes His favor has gone before me, causing deals to supernaturally close quickly. And sometimes, He's navigated me to avoid situations that would have otherwise bogged my schedule for days and weeks. Trust me, God is a rewarder of those who diligently seek Him.

Seek His face early and often. It's not about a specific program or even a particular amount of time, it's a lifestyle. As often as we breathe, we can be aware of Him. As often as we eat food, we can be feeding our souls with the meditation of a scripture. God is all around us, abiding with us in every moment of every day, and He's just waiting for us to engage with Him.

Trust Him with your time. You'll soon discover you have more than you'll ever need!

NOTES

WEEK 20:
THE BATTLE OF THE THORNS

As for what was sown among thorns, this is he who hears the Word,
but the cares of the world and the pleasure and delight and
glamour and deceitfulness of riches choke and
suffocate the Word, and it yields no fruit.
Matthew 13:22 (AMP)

The Parable of the Sower is one of the most powerful truths Jesus communicates in the Gospels. In fact, when his disciples asked Him what this parable meant, Jesus said to them, "If you can't understand the meaning of this parable, how will you understand all the other parables?" (Mark 4:13) With this answer in mind, I'd say it's pretty important we as Kingdom Builders study and meditate the many pearls of wisdom offered in this parable.

One of these truths, I like to call "The Battle of the Thorns," and it's been a cornerstone of wisdom throughout my life. And I'd venture to say, for the Christian who is pressing in to live a God-centered life, this battle of the thorns is what we struggle with on a day-to-day basis. It all comes down to this: Are we going to keep our hearts and minds focused on the Word and what God deems as important, or are we going to become distracted by the worries of this world? The writer, Matthew, even goes on to describe these distractions as "the pleasure and delight and deceitfulness of riches."

Is there anything in your life that is "choking out the Word" in your heart? These are worries that tempt you to doubt the promises of God. It's caring more what people think about you than what God thinks about you. It's anytime your desire for success and/or possessions tempts you to circumvent God's principles in order to attain them. It's putting your value in your position, your relationships, or your works rather than in who you are in Christ.

Every Kingdom Builder needs to be on the lookout for the thorns that invariably creep up in the soil of our hearts. And make no mistake: the more success you encounter, the more the thorns will magically appear. Make sure to keep a large bottle of Holy Spirit "Roundup" to squirt at these destiny-killing weeds. Stay girded up in prayer to recognize and prevent them from choking out your legacy!

NOTES

WEEK 21:
A KING'S SECRET FOR STRENGTH

And David was greatly distressed; for the people spoke of stoning him, because the soul of all the people was grieved, every man for his sons and for his daughters: but David encouraged himself in the LORD his God.
1 Samuel 30:6 (KJV)

Now here is a pearl of wisdom from a king, if ever there was one. In 1 Samuel 30, we find King David in the worst possible scenario. He and his mighty men have just returned home from battle only to find it in ruins. The Amalekites have burned the entire city of Ziklag and have kidnapped every single person. All of the men's wives, children, friends and families are gone! The entire company was so devastated that they wept 'until they had no more power to weep.'

Then, just as we thought it could not get any worse for David, all the men began to focus their grief upon him by planning to stone him! So not only was David grieved beyond words for the loss of his family, but now he had to deal with the betrayal of his entire company of soldiers. I think we can all agree that our darkest day still pales in comparison to this. But watch what this man of God, this authentic Kingdom Builder, did next: he strengthened himself in the Lord his God.

David didn't get defensive against his men as they blamed him for their losses, he didn't crawl up in a ball and give up, and most of all, he didn't shake a fist at his God and cry, "Why me, God? Why are you doing this to me?" Not even close. He recognized the situation he was facing was impossible from every angle and that he needed help from the only One who could make all things possible. He fell to his face before His God and renewed his strength and courage in Him. Once his spirit was quieted, David was able to hear the wisdom about what to do next. And guess what? David and his men recovered ALL that was stolen, from the least to the greatest.

My friend and partner in building God's Kingdom, whatever situation you might be facing today, no matter how impossible the solution might seem, I encourage you to run to your Father in heaven and surrender the entirety of the issue to Him. Strengthen yourself in your God through prayer, praise and worship, and pursuit of His Word. And your spirit will become your path and whisper strategy into your heart that will enable YOU to recover ALL the enemy might be trying to steal from you. With God on your side, who can be against you?

Trust and Believe!

NOTES

WEEK 22:
COURSE CORRECTION

And let us not lose heart and grow weary and faint in acting nobly and doing right, for in due time and at the appointed season we shall reap, if we do not loosen and relax our courage and faint.
Galatians 6:9 (AMPC)

At one point or another, all kings struggle with some level of lust, materialism, greed, ego, control, and self-ambition. I am no exception, and my prayer is this very transparent testimony will encourage and bring correction, if need be.

No matter where we are at in our character, God loves us and is ever reaching out to pull us into His perfect will for our lives. But sometimes this cannot happen without a course correction. For me, this gentle-but-strong correction came from God through my amazing wife. Laura is a true prayer warrior and her intercession for me saved me when I was at critical crossroads in my walk with the Lord. After a full night of praying, God gave her this word for me:

"The gifting is the ability to make money and friends or acquaintances easily. The fruit of that is sowing money into the Kingdom – which is most obvious – But what I have believed the greater Gift or Treasure that God has given you is the connection with these "influential people," not to be "schmoozing" or rubbing egos in the flesh, but for you to influence these people with your testimony of God's grace for the Lord. The huge amount of grace God has given you in that area – Be careful not to lose your testimony or "saltiness." You have been through tremendous trials and tribulations that God has supernaturally protected you through. You have overcome the snares of the enemy of materialism, lust of the flesh (all kinds), making yourself king and your business lord of your life, obsession with your image and position in life. All of these (snares) are aborting your plan that the Lord had for your life...which was to be in a position to be able to speak directly into the lives of men who may be ensnared in the same areas that God has given you grace in – and also supernatural insight to their specific situation and the lies of the enemy they are believing. Do not push or talk God off the throne of your life – allow Him to remain King and He will provide and protect you – as He gives grace to the humble and resists the proud. I love you with all my heart! Do not grow weary of doing good – for the Lord wants to see you grow to full maturity and love in the Lord. - Laura"

I needed these words more than I knew. And God reprioritized my heart, with Him as King. Is there any unhealthy area you need to deal with? Prayerfully ask God if you need a course correction.

NOTES

WEEK 23:
OLD BUT STILL KICKING

Those who are planted in the house of the Lord Shall flourish in the
courts of our God. They shall still bear fruit in old age;
They shall be fresh and flourishing,
Psalm 92:13-14 (NKJV)

I don't know about you, but I'm in this race to finish strong. When I'm "old" (whatever that means), I want the younger people around me to say, "Look at that guy. He might be old, but he's still got game!" This scripture gives us a secret to the true fountain of youth: involvement in the local church.

The local church is vital to every Kingdom Builder's mission and success. First of all, if we are not planted in a church, then what kingdom are we building? Never forget that Jesus promised us that the gates of hell would not prevail against the church. (Matt. 16:18) He didn't say the enemy would not prevail over our families, or our businesses, or our lives. The only way we can be assured the gates of hell will not prevail over us is when we are involved in and committed to a local church.

In our tech-savvy environment, we can get all kinds of teaching from almost any preacher we want. Today it's possible to have a virtual church experience each week and never get out of bed. But this isn't the fullness of what Jesus is talking about here. The original Greek word for "church" in this scripture means "a gathering of people." Church is not just getting good teaching or watching a service online. It's actually getting involved with a gathering of people so that we can minister to each other, serve each other, and pray for each other. It's by engaging with a local church that we stay connected and continue to flourish, as the scripture above teaches.

I completely understand how busy our lives can be and how relaxing it can feel to stay at home every Sunday. But this is not God's way. Sure, we can feel refreshed for a moment, but that refreshment is fleeting. However, when we trust God's way, and come to His house, we actually find true rest and refreshment for our souls. And even though our bodies might grow old, being involved in our church will keep our vision fresh and young. More importantly, it is a great legacy to pass on.

Renew your passion for your local church. Serve there. Give there. Pray there. Build there. Make it be a nonnegotiable part of your Kingdom Builder lifestyle.

NOTES

WEEK 24:
MOTIVATED BY GOD

*Then I observed that most people are motivated to success
because they envy their neighbor. But this, too,
is meaningless—like chasing the wind.*
Ecclesiastes 4:4 (NLT)

When I first started out in business, I ran toward success like my hair was on fire. I wanted to be the best, the biggest, the richest. I worked more hours per day than not, and even in my sleep, I would analyze my strategies and business plans. Sure enough, I climbed the entrepreneurial ladder of success quickly, only to feel empty and insecure. Not to mention, once I hit the top, I had an even quicker plummet to the bottom.

The major reason my first attempts to find success were riddled with ups and downs, both financially and emotionally, was because I was motivated by all the wrong things. I wanted to be like someone else, or even worse, I wanted to be better in business than someone else. I was motivated by my own emptiness inside, desperately hoping my outward success would fill my inward need to find significance.

It was not until I got my heart right with God, and learned to value what He values, that my life balanced out, and my pursuit for success was exactly the opposite of "chasing the wind." When my true motive was to build God's Kingdom and be a blessing to someone else, things began to "work," and not just in my business, but in my personal and spiritual life as well.

Friend, take a moment today to stop and evaluate your motives. Search your heart. What are the driving forces that propel you to reach for success? Ask your spouse and close friends what they see in you. Any other motivation that is not from God will only bring stress, toil, and hardship. And even if you do reach monetary success, the rewards will be bitter. I remember a pastor years ago saying, "Even if you win the rat race, you're still a rat." Learn to love what God loves. Let your pursuits be God's pursuits. Become motivated by what motivates God. In doing so, you will find more peace and fulfillment than you ever thought possible!

NOTES

WEEK 25:
WHEN GOD, WHEN?

A faithful man shall abound with blessings, but he who makes haste
to be rich (at any cost) shall not go unpunished.
Proverbs 28:20 (AMP)

I hate waiting, especially when I am infused with a dynamic idea. I want to pray for a bit, and then I want to see that promise come to pass NOW! If God wants it done, then it should be done IMMEDIATELY, right? Besides, that's what prayer is for isn't it? And just about the time I start whining to God about why that promise hasn't materialized, He reminds me about those two things called faith and patience.

The truth is, seldom do the plans of God come to fruition as quickly as we want them to. God's timing is always perfect, even though His timeline is usually much longer than we are comfortable with. So then, what do we do? We think, "God must be busy at the moment; He probably would appreciate it if I just stepped in and help make things happen!" And we dive in and work our tails off to make that promise come to pass in our time frame.

But just as this proverb promises, when we make haste, even to accomplish God-ordained plans and "at any cost" strive to bring those plans to pass, we will not go unpunished. Usually that "punishment" is frustration and exhaustion because we are outside of God's grace and trying to accomplish the task on our own strength. But sometimes, in our haste, we can thwart the plans of God in our lives. Remember Abraham sleeping with his maidservant Hagar? (Genesis 16). It takes longer for the true promise to be fulfilled, not to mention the collateral damage that ensues.

Stay the course with God, trust His timing. Trust that your faithfulness to His time frame will bring results. Take it from me, you don't want to force the birthing of a God given promise in your life. Wait for it and God's abundant blessings will flow through your life, affecting generations to come!

NOTES

WEEK 26:
POSITION OF STRENGTH

The effective, fervent prayer of a righteous man avails much.
James 5:16 (NKJV)

I recall many years ago when I was getting some pants made, a tailor told me one leg was 3/4 inch shorter than the other. At first I didn't believe him. But then he showed me the measurements and told me that he saw this all the time. Because I had worn a thick wallet in my back pocket for years, this had actually caused my hips to shift and my leg to appear shorter. No wonder I had been dealing with frequent back pain. It took about a year, and a lot of stretching exercises, but eventually my legs returned to their original position.

When our bodies are stuck in a wrong posture, or if we are in a stagnant position for any length of time, we will become weak in that area. Our alignment gets off and pain will inevitably follow. Did you know this is true for our spiritual life as well?

When our position of prayer is "off," when we put this vital time with God at the bottom of our to-do list, we become weak in our spirit man. Just like my legs, our lives get out of alignment with the things of God, and after time, we feel disconnected to Him and we have a hard time hearing His voice.

The KEY to us not experiencing this "spiritual" atrophy is prayer. Everything in our lives needs to start and end with prayer. There just is no way around this. Prayer is what aligns us to the voice of God, to our destiny, and to our daily mission. Let's not allow a lack of prayer to cripple our walk, and dilute our influence in our family, business and church. Value prayer for its priceless power, and give time daily to it. In fact, put it FIRST every day. I promise you, you will never be the same if you are diligent to do so.

Henry Ward Beecher said, "The first hour is the rudder of the day— the Golden Hour." For years now, I have made this a priority, so I can personally assure you that you will be charged with a renewed faith, peace, and strength like never before. What is accomplished in this first hour is infinitely more beneficial than any task on your to-do list.

The position of prayer is the strongest you can take. Remember, a man cannot fall...when he's on his knees!

NOTES

WEEK 27:
BE A HERO OF FAITH

*But without faith it is impossible to please Him, for he who comes
to God must believe that He is, and that He is a rewarder
of those who diligently seek Him.*
Hebrews 11:6 (NKJV)

Hebrews 11 is one of my favorite chapters in the Bible because it is packed with some of the original Kingdom Builders in history. Many people call it the "Hall of Faith" because the writer talks about how all these heroes and their faith in God allowed them to lead lives that impacted, not only their generation, but also the millions that were to follow.

Also, over and over throughout this chapter we are given the blueprint formula for how to have the same kind of success in our own lives. Phrases like "by faith," "activated by faith," "motivated by faith," "actuated by faith," "guided by faith," and "prompted by faith" offer us strategies about how to approach every area of our destiny.

Let's just take one of these heroes: Noah. Here we have a guy who was the ONLY one, at that time, who believed in God. And when God asked him to do the absurd, Noah said "yes." Talk about faith! Can you imagine spending 60-70 years of your life publicly building a ridiculous structure for a purpose that had never been needed before, no doubt being ridiculed constantly by those around you? But Noah dealt with the loneliness and the hard labor by his faith in God. He was prompted, activated and guided by faith. Faith kept him diligently on task throughout the decades. And his faith ended up saving humanity.

ONE person's faith can change the world! I don't know about you, but I want to be included in heaven's "Hall of Faith," too. This means standing up for the promises God places in our hearts. It means using our faith to persevere through the challenges we will inevitably face in marriage, parenting, in business and in ministry. Even when it seems crazy to the world. It means standing in faith until we have stayed the course all the way to the finish line. Today, look for opportunities to be prompted, activated, motivated, actuated, and guided by your faith in God. This kind of faith is so pleasing to him AND it makes a difference.

NOTES

WEEK 28:
THE COMMANDMENT OF REST

Remember the Sabbath day, to keep it holy.
Exodus 20:8 (KJV)

When God first presented His people with the Sabbath day of rest, He didn't offer it simply as a suggestion. He made it a commandment, #4 of the Big 10. And it came with a punishment of excommunication, or worse, death. (Ex 31:14) I don't know about you, but I think God is very serious about us taking time to rest.

You might say, "Yeah, but isn't that under the Law?
We're under Jesus and a new Law of Grace." This is true, but the commandment of the Sabbath was only a reminder of the example God established at the foundation of the earth.

Remember, on the 7th day, He (GOD) rested, and this was not because the All-powerful Creator was tired. This Holy Sabbath was to imprint upon the hearts and minds of all of us the vital importance of our need to stop, rest, renew and recharge. And so it is today.

The only problem is, in the Christian world, so many of us have begun to view the Sabbath day of rest as a church service. We go to church and click "Sabbath" off our list. And while church is an important time for believers to come together to serve, mentor and celebrate what God has done, it cannot take the place of purposefully setting time aside to rest our minds, bodies and souls.

So what exactly is a Sabbath? It's a period of time that is regularly set aside: to rest, to seek God, to turn off from the world (yes, I mean TV, cell phones, and social media), and to fellowship with those people who are close to us. It's a time to take a deep breath without feeling guilty about all the tasks on our "Honey do" lists.

For many years, more than I'd like to admit, I blew this commandment off. Quite honestly, I didn't see the importance of it. And I paid a dear price for it. Without this discipline, I got cloudy in my vision, got full of my own wisdom, tried to make things happen, and made some mistakes that could have been prevented. Take it from me: learn to value the Sabbath, whatever that means for you. Keep it Holy. If you'll give God the time, He'll supernaturally renew and rejuvenate your spirit, soul and body! As a friend of mind told me recently, "Rest God's Way, not your way." Great advice.

NOTES

WEEK 29:
THE WORD IS THE ULTIMATE PEARL,
PART ONE

Every king or priest is on a journey toward fulfilling the vision God placed in his or her heart. Some are just getting started, and some have been forging forward for decades. No matter where you find yourself today, there is one absolute in your life that is vital in the lives of all legacy leaders and pastors, aka "kings and priests." It's THE weapon that can be wielded to defeat any obstacle or enemy, no matter how big or small, and it must be in your hand at all times. It's the Word of God.

I know many of you would say, "Lee, I've got that covered, so what's the next pearl?" But let me ask you this: Are you sure you've got that covered? Because if you're not speaking the Word over your life each and every day, your sword is hanging useless at your side. You've got to take that weapon out of its sheath and unleash its mighty power by opening your mouth, and with faith confess God's Word.

In the *Kingdom Builders Daily Confession,* I shared with you a powerful daily confession that I have prayed out loud for many years. Every king or priest must use his or her confession as a creative force to frame their world, to call those things that are not as though they were, and to wage war against the enemy. There is no substitute for a daily faith confession! Whether you need motivation to get out of a valley, or wisdom to know how to take your vision to the next level, or internal fortitude to withstand an attack from the enemy, these confessions will help move you forward into victory.

Kingdom Builder Strategy:

Commit to a time in the day that will be your declaration time. Set an alarm, save it in your PDA, tattoo it to your wrist, do *whatever* it takes for you remember it and stick to it. Stay consistent, and watch the Word begin to work things out in your life that you could never do on your own!

Kingdom Builder Meditation:

"I have the mind of Christ and hold the thoughts, feelings and purposes of His heart. I am a believer and not a doubter. I hold fast to the confession of faith. I decide to walk by faith and practice faith. My faith comes by hearing and hearing by the Word of God. Jesus is the Author and Developer of my faith."
(Rom 10:17; 1 Cor 2:16; Heb 4:14, 11:6, 12:2)

NOTES

WEEK 30:
THE WORD IS THE ULTIMATE PEARL,
PART TWO

One of the most common questions I field during business or ministry meetings is what I consider to be the most significant key for success. Without a question, my answer is: the Word of God. *Nothing* great or long-lasting can be built on any other foundation than the Word of God. As Kingdom builders, we must continually keep in mind that our top priority is the Word. Studying it, meditating upon it, and speaking it over our lives.

If we ever allow ourselves to become too busy to engage with the Word, then we have lost sight of Who the source of our strength is, and from where our success comes. We become wise in our own eyes, thinking "we've got this thing," when in actuality we are heading down a road that will eventually lead to self-destruction.

Let me challenge you today: For the next 30 days, carve several minutes out of each day to confess the Word of God over your life, your family, your business, and your ministry. Not simply as a discipline to check off your list and get on with your day, but to speak these words slowly and purposefully, mixing each scripture with your faith. I am confident that you will begin to experience an inner strength and peace that you've never had before. Your vision will grow, your confidence in God will deepen, and most importantly, your relationship with Jesus will become more intimate.

In the previous weeks declaration, I included part of the confession I have used for years, and I'm giving you the next section of it below:

"The love of God has been shed abroad in my heart by the Holy Spirit and His love abides in me richly. I keep myself in the Kingdom of light, in love, in the Word, and the wicked one touches me not. I fear not for God has given me a spirit of power, of love and of a sound mind. No weapon formed against me shall prosper. Every tongue that rises against me in judgment shall be shown to be in the wrong. God is on my side, I tread upon the serpents and scorpions and over all the power of the enemy. I take my shield of faith and quench every fiery dart. Greater is He who is in me than he that is in the world." (Ps 91:13; Is 54:17; Rom 5:5, 8:31; Eph. 6:16; 2 Tim 1:7; John 4:4,16, 5:18)

If you would like to read the entire Kingdom Builders Daily Confession, please see the back of the book.

NOTES

WEEK 31:
TWO ARE BETTER THAN ONE

Two are better than one, because they have a good reward for their labor. For if they fall, one will lift up his companion. But woe to him who is alone when he falls, for he has no one to help him up.
Ecclesiastes 4:9-10 (NIV)

True and Authentic Partnership. Yes, I know it's hard to come by, especially in the marketplace. And even more so when fame, money or great influence comes into play. All of a sudden people get amnesia and start acting crazy. But let me assure you, it's not God's plan for you to be a Lone Ranger out there without faithful and Godly partnerships. They are out there; you just need to mine them out.

I know what it's like to build a business with people around me who are only in it for their own personal gain. And thankfully, I've been blessed to build businesses with true and authentic partners who believe they are in God-ordained covenant relationship with me. Let me tell you, there is no comparison. The first breeds insecurity, confusion and greed. The second fosters trust, creativity, and exponential forward movement for the Kingdom of God.

Chris, one of my closest friends and valued partners in business and ministry, has been in covenant with me for almost 20 years. He has been a blessing to me and we've been through the thick and thin of pioneering several huge successful (and a few not so successful) projects. His abundance supplies for my lack and vice versa. However, alongside those endeavors came conflict and disagreements. But Chris and I knew God had ordained this relationship; therefore, divorce is not an option. We are always diligent to deal with these issues in their infancy. To protect ourselves from it becoming a major collateral issue, and in the end, it always made our partnership stronger.

Let's be wise enough to understand the vital element of true and authentic partnerships. But there's a price for this. You'll need to seek God so He can reveal to you those allies in your midst. You will need to be transparent and expose your warts! (Everyone has them.) And you'll need to be open to hear other ideas and strategies that — wait for it— might be more productive than yours! Sometimes these costs will hurt you, but it's usually just against your own ego. You will never regret the cost. The reward of having a few kings beside you as you go into the battlefield of the marketplace is unmatched.

NOTES

WEEK 32:
SHAKE IT OFF!

And let us not grow weary while doing good, for in
due season we will reap if we do not lose heart.
Galatians 6:9 (NKJV)

One of the greatest lessons of LIFE was taught to me by my son, Ashton, better known as "Nugget." When he was only 8 years old, I ran for a seat in the Louisiana Senate. This was probably one of the most grueling endeavors I'd ever embarked upon, as we pledged to go door-to-door to over 27 thousand homes! On many of these very long days in this epic journey, Nugget would come with me and spread his contagious charm to everyone he met. It was late in the afternoon, we must've knocked on hundreds of doors that day, and we came to a particular house that was, let's just say, less than cordial. The man shouted some very choice words at us, told us he hated politicians, and slammed the door in our faces.

I was livid. No one talks like that to my son, I thought! I wanted to go back in there and lay hands on that man, and I don't mean to pray for him. Nugget just looked up at me and said, "Dad, sometimes ya just gotta shake it off and keep going. Let's go get another house." I wanted to refute him, but one look at his genuinely happy face made me stop in my tracks. He was just so excited to be out with his Dad, helping me try to achieve an enormous goal. He was single-focused, and didn't have time for the distraction of offense or discouragement. Wow. Out of the mouth of babes.

In ministry and in the marketplace, we will face adversity. It's inevitable when we are pursuing God-sized visions. But know this: the enemy is watching and waiting for when those moments hit so he can try and convince us to get offended, to fly off the handle (like I almost did that day), or to just give up. But we need to take a lesson from Nugget and just "shake it off!" We need to be so excited to be out with our Father, helping Him to achieve enormous goals for His Kingdom. If we will keep our eyes on that, just like Nugget, we won't have time for the distraction of anger, offense, or discouragement.

Be encouraged. No matter what you are facing today in your life, your marriage, your family, your ministry, or doing things God's way, you have this promise: You will reap a harvest, if you do not lose heart and give up.

NOTES

WEEK 33:
COUNT THE COST

For which of you, intending to build a tower, does not sit down
first and count the cost, whether he has enough to finish it—
lest, after he laid the foundation, and is not able to finish,
all who see it begin to mock him,
Luke 14:28-29 (NKJV)

Plan before you act. Jesus took the time during his earthly ministry to impress this vital discipline, in many different ways, into the hearts and minds of his followers. The scripture above is just one of these times. He knew that the leaders around him had the boldness to take on the call of spreading the Gospel with great tenacity. But he also knew these Type A personalities could leap before they think...Shoot—Fire—Aim! Sound like anyone you know?

So many of us are great at diving in. We're full of vision and we love a new challenge. But do we always stop and count the cost beforehand? I have seen too many men and women (including myself) take off sprinting like wildfire at the starting line, gain huge success quickly, but then implode before reaching the first mile marker. We'll never glorify God and reach our full potential if we live like this. We must learn to count the cost—in all matters—and weigh things out carefully before we act. Here are some checks and balances every Kingdom builder must have in place:

1) Is what you are pursuing God-ordained? Are you certain it's God-breathed and not man-breathed? You never want to have to complete a project in your own strength, so if you've thought it up on your own, then guess what? You're going to have to finish it on your own. Make sure your business, marriage, and life plans are congruent with God's plan for your life.

2) Are you in one accord with your spouse? Never go forward in ministry or business if you are not in full agreement. Have the patience to pray and seek God until you both are on the same page. No matter how long it takes.

3) Do you have wise counsel around you? And I'm not talking about the "guy" next door whom one time "back in the day" thought of doing what you're doing. Never consult anyone who doesn't have an historical success record. You can never get a person with a "3x5" index card experience level to help you with a billboard-size opportunity. Humble yourself and get a small group of wise people who have successfully gone where you want to go, pursue them and glean as much wisdom as you can!

These three vital keys will help you count the cost and stay on course!

NOTES

WEEK 34:
POST VICTORY PLAN

*Be sober, be vigilant; because your adversary the devil walks about
like a roaring lion, seeking whom he may devour.*
1 Peter 5:8 (NKJV)

Most people who reach a certain level of success, in any area of life, didn't attain that success accidentally. Whether it be in business, in ministry, in finances, and even in relationships, if we've had the privilege of experiencing a "win," most likely we had a strategy for how we got there. We planned, we researched, we received counsel, and hopefully, we prayed fervently for the wisdom of God. But my question to you is this: have you taken as much time and effort to strategize a POST-victory plan of attack?

Many times, as we are climbing up the mountain of success, our eyes are so focused on the prize that we naturally filter out those things that could distract us or be harmful to us. We simply don't have the time to dabble in the sin that lurks around us. But after we reach the top of the mountain, it's a whole different story. We stop to celebrate (which we should), but sometimes we also relax and let our spiritual guards down. And if our success was public in any way, maybe we begin to relish in all the wonderful things our "fans" and the media are saying about us. Maybe we even begin to believe the lie that we are set and nothing could possibly knock us off our mountain of success. And then we are in the perfect position for the attack of the enemy.

Take it from me; the moment you reach success or have a mountaintop experience, buckle up! Be alert and very sober minded, because the devil is watching and he loves to take people out when they are on the top. Make sure, in all your pre-success planning, that you also take the time to strategize a post-victory plan. Here are some ideas to get you started:

1) Get on your knees before God. After any victory, big or small, remember it was GOD who gave you the ability to reach success. Dig deeper in prayer as you spend extra time with your Father, thanking Him and giving Him all the glory.

2) Take any media attention with a grain of salt. Never forget for a second the media is your new BFF. Always proceed with extreme caution in any involvement with the press.

3) Take time to make sure your marriage and family are taken care of. If your recent endeavor has required large commitments of your time, it's time to sow into your spouse and your kids. No level of success is worth sacrificing these relationships.

NOTES

WEEK 35:
EXCELLENCE: THE BEST WITNESS

And this I pray, that your love may abound still more and
more in knowledge and all discernment, that you may
approve the things that are excellent.
Philippians 1:9-10 (NKJV)

As a marketplace or church ministry leader, the best witness
we can offer the 21st century world is to operate in all we do with a
spirit of excellence. If we have a desire to represent Jesus in our
churches and businesses, then be excellent. You are not helping His
Cause if you are flaky, unorganized, poor stewards of personal or
corporate income, always looking for the short-cut, and not holding
true to your words or commitments. What does it say about our
awesome Lord if we claim to be Christians but operate business-as-
usual in a second-rate way?

Rather than displaying a Jesus fish on all our marketing
materials, let's just run our businesses with such excellence and
integrity that the world around us cannot help but stop and take notice.
When we are honest in our dealings, excellent in our pursuits, and
accountable to what we have been blessed to steward, we will
automatically become representatives of our excellent Savior and God.
People will come to us for advice about how they, too, can reach our
levels of success with such authority.

And if I may go a bit deeper...living with a spirit of excellence
more importantly applies to your private life. Are you treating your
covenant of marriage with excellence? Are you parenting with
excellence? When you are alone, are you spending your free time in a
healthy manner? Examine yourself and your life, and take
responsibility for the areas you know you have been flaky or have
compromised. Make a quality decision to start now bringing excellence
into everything you do.

Please understand that excellence does not mean perfection.
Nobody is perfect. Excellence simply means that your heart is open to
God in all things, that you allow integrity to guide you, and you do your
best to walk with the Spirit of God. If you desire to be an ambassador
for Christ, then choose excellence every day. Ask God to help you. And
remember, His Spirit, which is the source of all excellence, lives on the
inside of you. So be encouraged YOU can be excellent!

NOTES

WEEK 36:
FIRE YOURSELF!

*For what will it profit a man if he gains the
whole world, and loses his own soul?*
Mark 8:36 (NKJV)

Have you ever had one of those moments when your child says something to you in passing and it absolutely penetrates your heart? For me, it was several years ago, and my precious daughter, Bella, was sitting on my lap. She must have been only 4 or 5 at the time. She looked up at me and said, "Daddy, aren't you the boss of your company?" When I told her I was, she said, "then I think you should fire yourself because we don't get to see you very much." OUCH! Those words exposed my heart so deeply! And I knew I needed to make changes. Immediately.

Trust me when I say, I completely understand how easy it is to get caught up with building our ministry and our business to the point that we are putting in 60-80 hour work weeks. This means we are only putting a few hours a week into our families. We are intoxicated by the next deal, the higher level, the greater influence because we are addicted to the rush of success. It feels so good to achieve great things!

The only problem is, how long will we enjoy the money, the influence, and the success if we've lost our marriage along the way? If our relationships with our kids is estranged? If we are all alone? What will it profit you if you gain all the success of the world, but your soul is sick because you've lost everything in the world that really matters?

After Bella's comments pierced my heart, I took a brutal assessment of my life and my schedule. I made some decisions that made me feel like I was dying to myself, which indeed I was. I was dying to my own ambition and my own striving. But in exchange I gained such a higher prize! And let me say that there is nothing more fulfilling than living out a healthy marriage with my amazing wife, and sharing a close relationship with all of my kids.

If you are spending way too much time away, whether actually at the "office" or being mentally "checked out" when you are at home, FIRE YOURSELF! Balance your time and realign your priorities. And when you leave the office leave all the issues there, too. Don't take them home and dwell on them all night long. The greatest present you can ever give to your family is your presence.

NOTES

WEEK 37:
WHAT'S THE GRUDGE?

For if you forgive other people when they sin against you, your heavenly Father will also forgive you. But if you do not forgive others their sins, your Father will not forgive your sins.
Matthew 6:14-15 (NKJV)

Who are you fighting? Who are you holding a grudge against? Many of us have offenses stored in our hearts like boxes in our attic. We know they're there, we can read the label of their contents, and there is that nagging feeling we probably should clean them out. In addition, if we were to be brutally honest about those boxes, we couldn't really verify exactly what is inside them, unless of course we opened them up and sifted through the details.

Unforgiveness is a lot like this. Just boxes of offense cluttering up our hearts, taking up space in our lives, in our minds and our emotions, and robbing us of having a clear vision for our destiny. All of us have had people who betrayed us, used us, and done us wrong. But instead of harboring those old wounds, re-opening them by reminding ourselves about how wrong those people were, we need to simply let them go. It's a colossal waste of time to allow someone else to keep us from everything God has for us. Many times these people don't even know we are mad at them! So in essence, your unforgiveness is keeping YOU in bondage while the person runs free. What if you just put an end to the grudge match and chose to forgive instead?

Jesus paid a dear price for the sins of the entire world.
That means your sins, all you have done and even those you will ever do, are completely wiped clean. And it means all the sins of the person who hurt you are forgiven too. So, let's get into agreement with the One whom you call your Lord and Savior, and ask Him to help you forgive completely and unconditionally. Just as He did for you.

If you've got offense stored in your heart, it's time to let it go and let it drop. The battle is the Lord's! That match is over, and you have the ability to win over bitterness and strife. Let's clean out our hearts so we can be free to fight the real fight. The fight of faith!

NOTES

WEEK 38:
PREACH NAKED

*So here's what I want you to do, God helping you: Take
your everyday, ordinary life—your sleeping, eating,
going-to-work, and walking-around life—and place it
before God as an offering. Embracing what God
does for you is the best thing you can do for him.*
Romans 12:1 (MSG)

It's easy to "look" holy in church. No matter what happened throughout the prior week, or even in hours just before church starts, we are pros at putting on our "Happy Christian" veneer, and greeting everyone with smiles and churchy language. But is this the real you? Are you giving great Godly advice to others, while in secret you aren't standing true to those words? Or, are you bragging about your latest successes in the marketplace while your family life is struggling? Or, do you find yourself smiling and laughing on the outside while you feel like you're dying on the inside? Habits like these will eat us up on the inside like a cancer devours a body.

We must learn to be transparent, hence the title "Preach Naked." I'm not saying we should walk around telling every single person we meet the details of all our negative situations, thoughts or emotions. But I am challenging us all (yes, that includes me) to live a life of transparency. To live the kind of life that is placed before God as an offering. We can't be ambassadors for God if we are being fake with everyone around us...even ourselves. My dear friend, Pastor Rick Bezet, wrote a great book about being you titled "Be Real: Because Fake Is Exhausting." We need to be who we truly are and stop trying to be someone we secretly know we are not. Transparency is key for a healthy marriage, for long-term relationships with our kids and with friends, and for true success in business. It's also one of the most important character traits for leaving an honorable legacy.

This week, be aware of those times in your everyday life—your going-to-work and walking-around life—where you feel yourself hiding behind a mask. Whether it's to impress someone else, or to hide secret sin, or it's just out of insecurity, take note when you find yourself in these situations.

Later, pray and ask God to help you trust Him enough with every aspect of your life that you never have to act fake. Talk to your spouse or a trusted friend, and practice being completely transparent. Transparency builds trust in all your relationships: marriage, kids, friends, and business. If you will learn to live transparently, as an offering before God, you will never need to be "fake" again, even when you go to church.

NOTES

WEEK 39:
ALL ABOUT THEM?

*When you reap the harvest of your land, you shall not wholly
reap the corners of your field, nor shall you gather the gleanings
of your harvest. And you shall not glean your vineyard,
nor shall you gather every grape of your vineyard; you shall
leave them for the poor and the stranger: I am the Lord your God.*
Leviticus 19:9-10 (NKJ)

This scripture is the heartbeat of the Kingdom Builder. We love the harvest, but not simply because we want to take it all for ourselves. In fact, it's quite the opposite: we love the harvest because we are so full of God's vision to help people, that we cannot wait to use our resources to build the Kingdom of God! We understand that God's way is never to meticulously hoard every last grape for ourselves. This kind of selfishness eventually begins to blind us, narrowing our sights to only our immediate needs, and eventually destroying us.

I love how God finishes this command with "I am the Lord your God" as if to say, "Regarding this command, you will be accountable to Me." Not only that, I think God is also reminding us that when we live generously in this way, we become examples for Him; we are living lives that glorify and bring honor to Him.

Let's make sure to carry the spirit of this verse to all areas of our lives. When you take time to pray, are you using up all the minutes just to talk to God about yourself and your needs? When you meet with friends, are you bored unless the conversation is only about things that pertain to or are interesting to you? In your marriage, are you mostly concerned with how your spouse is treating you? Do you glean your schedule to the very edges in your field of time, or do you have margin built in for when you notice the person around you who needs help?

In other words, how much of your life is all about YOU? When you take the time and resources to help someone else, to think about another's need, to reach out selflessly to your spouse or kids, you will truly begin to live in a supernatural harvest from God. He will fill you, not simply with monetary gain, but also with a deep satisfaction, joy, and abundant peace in your very soul. Remember, when you help others reach their dreams, God will give you the secret dreams of your own heart.

Live BIG. Live for OTHERS!

NOTES

WEEK 40:
PASTORS SET THE TABLE

And have made us kings and priests to our God;
And we shall reign on the earth.
Revelation 5:10 NKJV

Pastors are gifted by God to possess great vision, a supernatural ability to see far-reaching strategies for influencing the lost and discipline the saints. In fact, these visions are so exciting, they can keep them up at night...one, because they are so fired up to see God working through them and their church, and two, because they have no idea how God is going to provide all the resources needed in order to implement these great plans! But here's one thing they (and you) can always count on: If God gave you the vision, He will always supply the PRO-vision.

That provision is sitting right in front of the pulpit. It's the business leaders who attend their church, many of whom are trying to medicate the pain of the discontentment they are feeling through destructive behaviors. They thought success would bring the fulfillment and validation they were searching for, but the money and the influence only left them wanting more. This is because they have never connected to their true Kingdom purpose. They're longing to invest their lives into a God-purposed destiny, and pastors hold the key that will unlock this door.

When a businessperson connects to Kingdom purposes, everything changes! These men and women are awakened to their own new visions and strategies, and their resources flourish like never before. The result? Churches get built and paid for. The Gospel goes forth and more lives are saved. Missions are sent, the poor are fed, the oppressed are helped, and our communities are transformed, all in Jesus' name.

Simply put, pastors need business people, and vice versa. These two destinies are indelibly intertwined and designed like this by God. We all need to understand the value of each other's calling and how important and powerful it is that we come into covenant.

The first thing pastors must come to understand is no matter how brilliant or successful marketplace leaders are, they absolutely need YOU to invite them to the table of this covenant. Not only are they looking to you for spiritual leadership, but they also understand authority, so most of them would never usurp a pastoral lead. They need to be invited and pastored so they can understand THEIR value to the vision God has placed on the church.

Secondly, pastors and business leaders must take time to understand each other and to learn each other's language. Or as I like to say, we need to interpret each other's dialect. We are like the Chinese language in many mays. They are both called "Chinese," but the Mandarin dialect and the Cantonese dialect are very different! So many times in the church, the business leaders are speaking Mandarin while the pastors are speaking Cantonese...but we both believe we are speaking Chinese. And we wonder why sometimes we miscommunicate. It's simply because we need to learn each other's dialect. This is done by a consistent effort by all to build authentic and transparent relationships.

Pastors hold the key to unlock this dynamic partnership that will advance the cause of the local church. If we really believe that the local church is the hope of the world, we must realize this will never happen if we don't equip and empower our modern-day kings to charge into battle. Side by side, pastors and business people will become a force of epic proportions and we will be the hope AND the change our world is crying out for.

NOTES

WEEK 41:
WHO ARE YOU LISTENING TO?

*Blessed (happy, fortunate, prosperous, and enviable) is the man
who walks and lives not in the counsel of the ungodly [following
their advice, their plans and purposes], nor stands [submissive and
inactive] in the path where sinners walk, nor sits down [to relax
and rest] where the scornful [and the mockers] gather.*
Psalm 1:1 (AMP)

Who are you listening to? What type of people are you hanging around? What sources are you using to get advice? These are crucial questions for every legacy builder to answer, and in that answering, be brutally honest. This verse in the Amplified Version is so descriptive, and at times, has really given me a gut-check to clean up the things and/or people speaking into my life.

As we run our businesses and ministries at 100 mph, it is so easy to lose track of who and what is speaking into our minds and hearts. Especially when those voices are full of the words, plans and predictions of what we want to hear. For some of us who tend to be people who are driven by anxiety and fear, it "feels good" to keep our ears inclined to the constant onslaught of negative news because it justifies our need to control, and our responsibility to worry. But God's simply not in that.

We can't let ourselves get comfortable in these voices and influences. Or, as the scripture above says, "to relax and rest" in ungodly arenas. These atmospheres will only cloud our thinking, and ultimately distance us from our one True Source: God.

If you've allowed yourself and your environment to become cluttered with negative news, social media, or input from ungodly people, it's time to clean house. Scrutinize the avenues from which you are receiving information daily. Get rid of the worldly static that is draining your ability to perceive what God is trying to say to you.

Only through clear channels from heaven can God's wisdom and blessing flow into your life and through your life!

NOTES

WEEK 42:
WHAT WAS HIS NAME?

And _____ took his son Abram and his grandson Lot, the son of
Haran, and his daughter-in-law Sarai, his son Abram's wife, and
they went out with them from Ur of the Chaldeans to go to the land
of Canaan; and they came to Haran and dwelt there. So the days of
_____ were two hundred and five years, and died in Haran.
Genesis 11:31-32 (NKJV)

If I were to ask you to give me the name of Abraham's father, could you fill in the blank? We all know who Abraham is. He is the father of many nations, literally! He is the father of faith for over half of the world's population: Christianity, Judaism, and Muslim. But what was the name of his father?

You might be wondering why I'm stuck on this piece of trivia, until you take a closer look at this scripture above. (By the way, the answer is Terah.) The Bible tells us that when Terah set out from Ur with his family, his intention was to go to the land of Canaan, the land of promise. But he never got there because he stopped short of his goal, and instead settled in Haran. He stopped short and he settled. And the next verse says he died there. As a result, now only Bible scholars can even recall his name. Today, we have many children named Abraham, but we are not seeing any mamas lining up to name their sons Terah!

This is a profound reality. God has put a dream and a vision in each of our hearts, and as Kingdom Builders, we are passionate to achieve those dreams so that we can leave a lasting legacy to future generations. But if we get weary, or grow doubtful, or give up before the promise comes to pass, we will abort the legacy God is trying to give us. If we settle for the mediocrity of Haran, and we never strive for Canaan, then we'll miss our chance to be and to do all that God has for us. We'll die in Haran. And then years later, our great-grandchildren will be saying, "Grandpa who? What was his name again?"

Keep going. Keep fighting. Keep pursuing the dreams God has gifted your vision with. No matter how long it takes, never settle in Haran. You were not made for mediocrity, and you are not destined to stop short of the promise land. You are a Kingdom Builder who was made in the likeness and image of God. You have the power of the Almighty God residing on the inside of you! He is on your side, and He is fighting for you.

Charge on and seize the promise!

NOTES

WEEK 43:
THE SECRET TO SUCCESS

*The generous soul will be made rich, and he
who waters will also be watered himself.*
Proverbs 11:25 (NKJV)

We all want the secret to success. Whenever I am out teaching about what it means to be a Kingdom Builder, I inevitably am asked to field this question: What is the key for financial success? Well, today, I'm going to tell you! The secret to finding success as a Kingdom Builder is giving. It's being generous, using everything God has blessed you with. And I'm not just talking about money. Being generous is so much more than writing a check. It's being open with your life, your wisdom, your time, your friendship, and your faith.

But probably the most challenging aspect of authentic generosity is that it's about giving FIRST, not waiting to receive, and then giving. Can you imagine if God had rested on His heavenly throne, and waited to receive our adoration for Him before He decided to send His Son into the world to die for us? We'd all still be waiting for the salvation of our souls! God gave FIRST, and it is only because of that act of immeasurable generosity that we have the privilege to give back to Him and to His Church.

The generous soul will be made rich. He who waters first, will then be watered. Stop thinking that you will start giving when the money starts pouring in. I promise you, it doesn't happen that way. If you cannot give the $100 tithe, there is no way you are magically going to be able to give the $10,000 tithe...let alone the $100,000 tithe! Start giving your resources, your wisdom, your time, and your love now and watch God work in every area of your life. Because when you give first, you are operating in the way you were created: in God's likeness and image.

Finally, always use these four checks to keep your generosity authentic: Generosity has no motive. Generosity requires no justification. Generosity needs no response. Generosity just does, because LOVE does!

NOTES

WEEK 44:
BY GOD, FOR GOD

For it was in Him that all things were created, in heaven and on earth, things seen and things unseen, whether thrones, dominions, rulers, or authorities; all things were created and exist through Him [by His service, intervention] and in and for Him.
Colossians 1:16 (AMP)

We were created by God, for God. Sometimes we get that twisted up, don't we? We think we were created by God, for us. Or that we have to create our own way, make our success happen for God. What a relief to let this truth sink in. We were created by God, for God. So all our striving can cease. All our worrying over whether or not we're going to make it can be silenced. If we were created by the Master of the Universe, for His plan and purpose, then certainly, all we need to do is get out of the way and trust in Him.

This sounds so easy and yet is so hard to do. We start to doubt that His timing is really the most productive. We begin to compare ourselves and our successes with another, and begin to wonder if maybe we need to step in and take charge. And sometimes, we can get so focused on the gifts and the progress of another that we make the choice to throw aside the dream that was originally in our heart and try to do what that other person is doing. We stop being who God created us to be as we attempt to create our own destiny.

I want to encourage you today. Exactly who you are is exactly who God made you to be. You were given a unique thumbprint by God, and He does not want you to be anything else. He's not wishing you were as smart as another, or as successful as another, or as funny, or as pretty, or as charismatic, or as daring, or as...or as...He made you to be you, and He likes it that way! Besides, trying to be someone you're not is a lost cause since you're just not going to be good at being someone else. My pastor friend, Rick Bezet, wrote a book entitled, "Be Real: Because Fake is Exhausting." How true is that? You were made by God for God. Embrace who you are. Stay in your lane. It is only when you are in the lane God created for you that you will find your purpose, and the provision for that purpose. Your success and your fulfillment in life will only be found in the lane God has fashioned specifically for you.

So get planted in your local church, where you can identify your lane and then put the pedal to the metal and DRIVE!

NOTES

WEEK 45:
THE ONLY ONE

For we are God's [own] handiwork (His workmanship), recreated in Christ Jesus, [born anew] that we may do those good works, which God predestined (planned beforehand) for us [taking paths which He prepared ahead of time], that we should walk in them [living the good life which He prearranged and made ready for us to live].
Ephesians 2:10 (AMP)

It is a profound reality that right now 7 BILLION people are living on our planet, and yet each person has a unique set of fingerprints. It's as if our Creator God was so committed to us knowing that every single one of our lives was significant, He permanently "tattooed" our uniqueness at the edge of our fingertips.

You are God's masterpiece, highly valued and strategically placed in this moment in time. God not only wants you to embrace the "you" He created, He greatly desires you to fulfill His purpose for your life. God did not create you just to trudge through an existence, hating your job, bored of your relationships, and feeling unfulfilled and dissatisfied. Not even close! He created you to thrive in this life, in every season!

If you are feeling "stuck" in any area of your life, I encourage you to dig deeper in your prayer time with God. Ask Him what you are missing, and how you can take steps to feel fully engaged and firing on all cylinders. Talk to a mentor, or a very close friend who believes in you. Share with your spouse your thoughts, and pray together as a powerful force of agreement to see your lives open up to ALL God has for you.

You are called for a purpose, and you are the only one who can fulfill that purpose. The world needs you, your family needs you, your church needs you, and YOU need you! Never settle for less than that "full" life which He prearranged and made ready for you to live.

NOTES

WEEK 46:
WHAT'S YOUR SCORECARD?

Do not love the world or the things in the world. If anyone loves the world, the love of the Father is not in him. For all that is in the world, the lust of the flesh, the lust of the eyes, and the pride of life is not of the Father but is of the world. And the world is passing away, and the lust of it; but he who does the will of God abides forever.
1 John 2:15-17 (NIV)

What is your scorecard for success? How do you measure your success? Is it once your business or your salary has reached a particular level? Is it the kind of car you drive or house you live in? What are the benchmarks that make you walk a little bit taller, shoulders a bit broader?

I think it is very easy, even for Christian marketplace leaders, to use a scorecard from the world's perspective to measure our success. The things of this world are easy to see, and they make our flesh feel important and satisfied. I know, because there was a long season of my life when I looked to the world to gratify my need for significance. Sure, I was a Christian and prayed and asked God to help me out spiritually. But as far as personal success went, it was much easier to find my level of importance by measuring how much money I had, how many wonderful things I'd provided for my family, and how much I'd given to the church.

However, at the end of the day, I still felt empty inside. It seemed like the more I had, the less clear my vision became. The more success I was able to juggle, the less peace I felt in my heart. I began to seek God fervently, and He showed me that even though my intentions were good, my motivations were still very much steeped in worldly thinking. I was still using a scorecard from the world's perspective to judge my success, instead of keeping my heart and my mind tuned in to the scorecard of Heaven. In essence, I was still loving what the world loved and not fully loving what God loved.

Did that mean that I sold everything and lived like a monk? Of course not! That's not what God was trying to show me. He was simply trying to help me get my heart in the right position to value what He valued, in every area of life. And once I began to let go of the world's scorecard, I was sincerely able to do the will of God for my life. And the crazy thing is, God blessed our family even more than before. But that was only because God knew He could trust us to steward it properly. When you love what GOD loves, only then will you truly know prosperity.

NOTES

WEEK 47:
SHARE THE PLATFORM?

Now after this the Lord chose and appointed seventy others and
sent them out ahead of Him, two by two, into every town
and place where He Himself was about to come.
Luke 10:1 (NIV)

Great leaders share their platform. Greater leaders are passionate about raising up the next generation of leaders. And the best leaders are those who are not afraid to replace themselves. Where do you fall in this spectrum? In the Old Testament, we see a leader who was not able to make room for the next great leader. King Saul was intimidated by David, even though God told him David would be the next king. Saul liked what David could do for him, but it stopped there. He wasn't about to give up his influence and authority to someone else. He even spent many years trying to hunt David down and kill him. King Saul was much more interested in building his own kingdom, not God's kingdom. And because of this disobedience, Saul left a legacy of insecurity and tragedy.

Jesus is the model for leadership, and He was not afraid to share His platform, as He gave His disciples the spiritual authority to go ahead of Him and do mighty works. Jesus was determined to raise up a band of leaders, because He knew they were going to have to carry the torch of the Gospel once His earthly ministry was over. And I love the scripture where Jesus reassures them that they would do greater works than He was able to do. (John 14:12) All of them collectively, filled with the Christ's power, would be able to influence more people than Jesus could as one person on the earth. How much more should this reality ring true in our own ministry, family, and business?

If you will follow Jesus' example and not Saul's, you will not only flourish, but those around you will be enabled to flourish as well. By empowering the next generation of leaders, you will foster a spirit of unity and synergy within your business and ministry. You and your team will accomplish exponentially more as a collective unit than you could ever accomplish on your own.

Share the platform. Empower those upcoming personalities. Lead to replace yourself. Be God's Kingdom Builder, rather than your own kingdom builder.

NOTES

WEEK 48:
LOCATION, LOCATION, LOCATION...
by: Jerry Meek

And so, dear brothers and sisters, I plead with you to give your bodies to God because of all he has done for you. Let them be a living and holy sacrifice—the kind he will find acceptable. This is truly the way to worship him. Don't copy the behavior and customs of this world, but let God transform you into a new person by changing the way you think. Then you will learn to know God's will for you, which is good and pleasing and perfect.
Romans 12:1-2 (NLTSB)

We live in the beautiful Sonoran Desert and many people are surprised that we have mountains and amazing views. It is always exciting walking a property with a client to determine if this is "the one." What are the advantages of this site? Are there any obstacles? What views will I have? One of the most talented architects I have had the privilege to work with is adamant that views should not be axial but panoramic. It is best when views are discovered.

The site conditions are what I look at first. Is the soil expansive? Does a hillside project require blasting or additional heavy equipment? Once these elements are discussed, we start thinking about how to place the house on the site. What about the views? Will we be taking advantage of daylight and shading for the intense Arizona sun? Yes, you really can fry an egg on the sidewalk in the summer with 120-degree heat. Locating the house in the right spot is important. It mitigates obstacles, and in the end, avoids surprises and re-works. Are you in the right place in your life? So many times we want to know the future of our lives. Similar to the house, we want our views to be axial, but God wants us to discover the panoramic view of what is ahead. With that being said, what do you think about living for today?

The biblical principle is that we live in the present trusting in the Lord, daily living our lives for Him, and He will direct us and guide us towards what He wants us to do in the future. In other words, we live by faith, trusting in the Lord today. And through this process, God will prepare us for future service and get us to where He wants us. Therefore, if we are living in God's will today, we can also trust Him to take care of the future.

As you seek God, live today as if it is the first and last day of your life.

NOTES

WEEK 49:
WINNING BEING SECOND

Then Pharaoh took his signet ring off his hand and put it on Joseph's
hand... And he had him ride in the second chariot which he had;
and they cried out before him, "Bow the knee!"
So he set him over all the land of Egypt.
Genesis 41:42-43 (NKJV)

Joseph is arguably one of the most influential heroes in the Bible. Other than Jesus, King David, and Moses, Joseph has the most chapters dedicated to the dramatic telling of his complete biography. No matter where he went, he became the manager of the world around him: first Potiphar's house, then of his prison, and finally of Pharaoh's kingdom. Joseph is certainly someone to emulate in your life.

But have you noticed that Joseph never actually possessed any realm of which he managed? Each one of his executive officer positions was for an entity that he had not founded nor inherited. Joseph was always second in command and he was perfectly content to be so. In truth, his willingness to impeccably serve another man enabled him to be the salvation for all of Egypt and the peoples of the then-known world.

Unfortunately, many people are not satisfied unless they are in the first chariot. But if this is not God's will for your life, your lust for the first seat will destroy you. Even if, like Joseph, you are serving an ungodly leader, you can still fulfill your destiny by being faithful, honoring, and thankful, and you might possibly change a nation. Embrace the gift God has given you, humble yourself, and your talent will not only be valued, but doors of destiny will be opened to you.

And if you happen to be the head of your own company, you must realize God is still in the front seat. Remember to keep yourself submitted to Him. God has always been and always will be in the first chariot. This is a truth to which every Kingdom Builder must surrender. Only in this holy order will the fullness of God's true power begin to flow in every area of our lives.

NOTES

WEEK 50:
MORNING HEART CHECK

*Search me, O God, and know my heart; Try me, and know
my anxieties; And see if there is any wicked way in me,
and lead me in the way everlasting.*
Psalm 139:23-24 (NKJV)

One of my heroes, here on earth, is Hall of Fame Coach Bill McCartney. He is the former head football coach of the University of Colorado, and the founder of both Promise Keepers and The Road to Jerusalem. This man has blessed my life unlike any other. The standard by which he lives, is one of the most authentically Christ-like examples I have known, and I value him greatly as a mentor and friend. In one of his teachings, he humbly admitted that for forty years, during his morning prayer, he asks God to search his heart thoroughly and to show him anything in his life that needs to be taken to the feet of the cross. He said, "Every day without fail, I have to check my motives so my heart can be clean to accomplish the things God has for me to do."

It was very profound for me to hear Bill say this. My thought was, here is a guy, who for decades, has lived his life "all in" for Jesus, and still has to search his heart daily? How much more do I need to? The answer to this question, for every single one of us is "yes!" There is not one of us who is above checking our motives. Every. Single. Day.

Remember, our heart is deceitful above all things, (Jeremiah 17:9) and only by spending time in the holy presence of our Father can we see our motives for what they truly are. So many can serve others with a passion, but really their motive is selfish, seeking notoriety or approval from others. So many can liberally give of their finances, but really their motive is gaining influence. So many can give of themselves, but they are giving simply to get.

Pastors, leaders, business people, and parents, we must be careful not to manipulate and put up smoke screens as if it's all about others...when really, it's all about us. Only you can take your heart before God and ask Him to search it thoroughly. It's only in our quiet time with God that we can ask Him to speak to our hearts, and show us if there is any wicked way or wrong motive inside us.

I realize this is a battle until Jesus comes back. But if we are diligent, we can learn to live our lives as true servants, being SEARCHED by God, FED by His Word and then LED by His Spirit. In this we will truly glorify God!

NOTES

WEEK 51:
GOD OF THE SECOND CHANCES

If you, God, kept records on wrongdoings, who would stand a
chance? As it turns out, forgiveness is your habit,
and that's why you're worshiped.
Psalm 130:3 (MSG)

God is the God of the Second Chance! I can declare this confidently because I have experienced God's mercy and kindness as He has brought restoration in my life, even when I caused the destruction in the first place. That's how good our God is. And that's one of the reasons He is worshiped.

I want to encourage you today, if you find yourself in a place where you think you've failed beyond repair, or if you have dreams that you've let die. Maybe you feel like you're living a "Plan B" life, and there's no way God could give you "Plan A." Over and over throughout the Bible, we see God reaching out to our heroes of faith and offering 2nd, 3rd, even 4th chances when they've blown it themselves. Starting with Adam and Eve, to Abraham, Isaac and Jacob, to King David, to the generations of Israelites when one generation would honor God, and the next forget all about him. All the way to Peter and Paul in the New Testament and everyone in between, God renewed their dreams.

God has called you to be a Kingdom Builder, and he's not done with you yet. No matter what situation we face, if we will come to God with a heart of repentance and humility, He will work out restoration in our lives beyond what we can image. AND we are to help the Kingdom Builders around us find this same restoration, if and when they might fail.

As Christians, we must stop shooting our wounded by judgment, condemnation, and an unwillingness to reinstate those who have fallen. We need to extend the same 2nd Chance that God has extended to us numerous times. I have a pastor friend who made some mistakes and had to let go of the ministry he had built. But thank God, because he took ownership of his choices and diligently sought a path of forgiveness and long-term recovery, he was able to begin rebuilding. Yes, he had to give up his "Plan A" destiny, but because of his humility and proven faithfulness, God didn't give him a "Plan B." He honored him back with a brand-new "Plan A" destiny! God is that good and that able.

I am eternally grateful that when I have submitted my failures and shortcomings to God, He has been overwhelmingly faithful to grant me 2nd chances. No matter what you might be facing today...lay it before God. In sheer transparency, go before your God, and then talk about it with your spouse, mentors, and pastor. It might take time to recover that which was lost, but trust in God. As it turns out, "forgiveness is His habit."

NOTES

WEEK 52:
LIVE A LEGACY

Children's children are a crown to the aged, and
parents are the pride of their children.
Proverbs 17:6 (NIV)

One day (hopefully later and not sooner) your human life will be complete and you will be standing before your Father in heaven. What will be your legacy? What degree of impact will you have made on this earth? What will be the final words said about you at your funeral?

Honestly, these questions are a driving force behind my life. And I go over the answers regularly, because they serve as a litmus test for me, and lead me to answer these questions:

1) Am I prioritizing my schedule according to my values
2) Am I giving my all as a husband and a father?
3) Is the focus of the ministry God has blessed me with helping people?
4) What eternal difference are my efforts making?
5) Am I putting God first in everything that I do?

I know that if I honor God, put my family first, and stay focused on Kingdom Purposes, I will leave a legacy that will be 'the pride of my children,' as this Proverb promises.

Today, I challenge you to take a moment and ask yourself these questions. Maybe even imagine what kind of words you'd like said at your funeral. Then, with brutal honesty, assess those answers and make sure your life decisions right now are lining up with the legacy you are passionate to give to the next generation.

And then, when the day does finally come and we graduate to heaven standing face-to-face with our Father, we will be able to watch as He proudly announces to the entire cloud of witnesses,

"Well done, thou good and faithful servant!"

NOTES

CONCLUSION

I hope this 52 Week Kingdom Builder Devotional has encouraged, challenged and inspired you to step up into the lane God has for you. Each one of us has a God-given lane to run our race, and to fulfill what God has created us for. I encourage you to start Week One, and take the journey again for another year. I truly believe that when you do you will find additional insight, as the Holy Spirit gives you countless revelations for your life.

Stay in your lane,

Lee

KINGDOM BUILDERS DAILY CONFESSION

Jesus is Lord over my spirit, soul and body (Phil 2:9-11)

Jesus has been made unto me wisdom, righteousness, sanctification, and redemption. I can do all things through Christ who strengthens me (1 Cor 1:30, Phil 4:13)

The Lord is my shepherd. I do not want. My God supplies all my needs according to His riches in glory in Christ Jesus. (Ps. 23; Phil 4:19)

I do not fret or have anxiety about anything. I do not have a care. I dwell in the House of Prayer. (Phil 4:6; 1 Peter 5:6-7; Isa. 55:7)

I am the body of Christ. I am redeemed from the curse, because Jesus bore my sickness and carried my diseases in His own body. By His stripes I am healed. I forbid any sickness or disease to operate in my body. Every organ, every tissue, of my body functions in the perfection in which God created it to function. I honor God and bring glory to Him in my body. (Gal 3:13, Matt 8:17; 1 Peter 2:24; 1 Cor 6:20)

I have the mind of Christ and hold the thoughts, feelings and purposes of His heart (1 Cor 2:16)

I am a believer and not a doubter. I hold fast to the confession of faith. I decide to walk by faith and practice faith. My faith comes by hearing and hearing by the word of God. Jesus is the Author and Developer of my faith (Heb 4:14; Heb 11:6; Rom 10:17; Heb 12:2)

The love of God has been shed abroad in my heart by the Holy Spirit and His love abides in me richly. I keep myself in the Kingdom of light, in love, in the word, and the wicked one touches me not. (Rom 5:5; 1 John 4:16; 1 John 5:18)

I fear not for God has given me a spirit of power, of love and of a sound mind. No weapon formed against me shall prosper. Every tongue that rises against me in judgment shall be shown to be in the wrong. God is on my side. (2 Tim 1:7; Isa 54:17; Romans 8:31)

I tread upon the serpents and scorpions and all over the power of the enemy. I take my shield of faith and quench every fiery dart. Greater is He who is in me than he that is in the world. (Ps 91:13; Eph 6:16; 1 John 4:4)

I let the word dwell in me richly. He who began a good work in me will continue until the day of Christ. (Col 3:16; Phil 1:6)

I am delivered from this present evil world. I am seated with Christ in heavenly places. I reside in the Kingdom of God's dear Son. The law of the Spirit of life in Christ has made me free from the law of sin and death. (Gal 1:4; Eph 2:6; Col 1:13; Rom 8:2)

I hear the voice of the Good Shepherd. I hear my Father's voice, and the voice of a stranger I will not follow. I roll my works upon the Lord. I commit and trust wholly to Him. He will cause my thoughts to become agreeable to His will, and so shall my plans be established and succeed. (1 John 10:27; Prov 16:3)

I am a world overcomer because I am born of God. I represent the Father and Jesus well. I am a useful member in the body of Christ. I am His workmanship recreated in Christ Jesus. My Father God is all the while effectually at work in me to will and do His good pleasure. (1 John 5:4-5; Eph 2:10; Phil 2:13)

I am the righteousness of God in Christ Jesus. (2 Cor 5:21)

I am the head and not the tail. I am above only and not beneath. I am blessed when I go in and when I go out. (Duet 28:13; Duet 28:6)

The Lord is my light and my salvation. I let my light shine before men. They see my good deeds and praise my Father in heaven. I am like a tree planted by rivers of water, that bringeth forth fruit in my season; my leaf shall not wither; and whatsoever I do shall prosper. (Ps 27:1; Matt 5:16; Ps 1:3)

I have the mind of Christ. I cast down imaginations and every high thing that exalts itself against the knowledge of God. I bring every thought into captivity in obedience to Christ. I think on whatever is true, honest, just, pure and lovely, and on whatever is of a good report, and on any praise. My mind is stayed in the Lord Jehovah. I trust in the Lord. I am in perfect peace. (1 Cor 2:16; 2 Cor 10:5; Phil 4:8; Isa 26:3,4)

I dwell in the secret place of the Most High and I remain stable and fixed under the shadow of the Almighty whose power no foe can withstand. The Lord is my refuge and fortress. No evil shall befall me – no accident shall overtake me – nor any plagues or calamity come near my home. The Lord gives His angels charge over me, to accompany and defend and preserve me in all my ways of obedience and service. They are encamped around about me. (Psalms 91:1,2,10,11 AMP; Psalms 34:7)

Through skillful and godly wisdom is my house built, and by understanding it is established on a solid foundation. My house is securely built. Jesus is our cornerstone. As for me and my house we shall serve the Lord. (Prov 24:3-4; Luke 6:48; Acts 4:11; Josh 24:15)

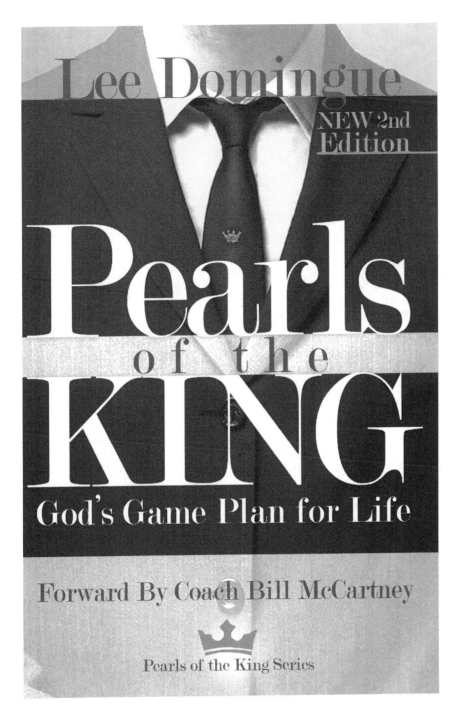

Visit www.kingdombuilders.us for more information.

ABOUT THE AUTHOR

Lee Domingue is an entrepreneur, international speaker, pastor, and author of Pearls of the King. His passion for the local church to be the hope of the world drives him to help pastors and business leaders understand just how vital they are to each other. Only by effectively developing an intentional relationship will they reach the potential of their God-given destinies. Through Kingdom Builders U.S. and serving as Legacy Pastor at Church of the Highlands in Birmingham, Alabama, Lee brings inspiration and practical strategies for pastors and business leaders to understand how dynamic their relationship can become to build the Kingdom of God.

Lee draws his messages from decades of success in business, dedicated study of God's Word, and committed service to his local church. In 1997, He founded AppOne, a financial technology company that was later acquired in 2007 by Wolters Kluwer, a multi-billion-dollar global information and compliance services company. After the acquisition, Lee worked as CEO – Indirect Lending until retiring in 2011 to focus his passion on Kingdom Builders U.S. and Trafficking Hope, the anti-human trafficking campaign he and his wife founded in 2007. Lee was Co-Executive Producer of anti-trafficking motion picture, CAGED NO MORE, which released in 2015.

At age 43, Lee was the youngest person to be named Business Report / Junior Achievement "Businessperson of the Year." In 2014, Lee and his wife Laura received the "Community Leaders of the Year" award for their work in fighting human trafficking from the Cenikor Foundation. Lee has served on various boards like A21 Campaign, Omni Bank, and Promise Keepers. Lee and his wife Laura have five children and two grandchildren.

For more information about Lee Domingue, Kingdom Builders, and Trafficking Hope visit: kingdombuilders.us

Made in the USA
Columbia, SC
20 April 2018